To my sister.

Thank you for choosing this book!

If what you read inspired you, helped you, or simply brought you joy, I warmly invite you to leave a review on the platform where you discovered this book.

Your feedback is invaluable! Not only does it help guide other readers in their choices, but it also allows me to keep sharing ideas and writing with passion. Every review matters and helps this book reach those who might truly need it. **By leaving a comment, you become a true part of this journey.** Thank you from the bottom of my heart for your support and for taking a moment to share your experience!

Introduction

Introducing the book's objective: Merging the Law of Attraction with the Scrum framework to achieve your dreams.

You've had a brilliant idea before. A burning desire. That moment of pure momentum, when everything feels possible. And then... nothing. Routine took over, and the dream was left hanging.
This book is for you. It won't ask you to choose between dreaming and doing. It will teach you how to do both.

Why is a new approach necessary?

At some point, we all feel that tension between our dreams and reality. You have deep aspirations, exciting ideas... but they often seem out of reach.
Motivation fades, projects stall, and daily life takes over again.

But what if you could finally align your desires with a clear method to make them real?

This book answers a fundamental question:
How to combine the power of positive thinking with an effective action method to turn your dreams into achievable goals?

A unique method: inspiration + structured action

The **law of attraction** encourages us to cultivate positive thoughts, clarify our intentions, and visualize our success. It's a powerful tool to create energy aligned with what we deeply desire.
But inspiration alone is not enough. Without a method, our dreams can remain vague ideas.

This is where the **Scrum framework** comes in: an agile methodology used in the professional world to manage complex projects. It allows you to move forward step by step, adapt to the unexpected, and turn a vision into concrete reality.

By combining these two approaches, this book offers you:

1. To use the law of attraction to clarify your desires, visualize your successes, and overcome your mental blocks.
2. To apply Scrum's agile tools to structure, prioritize, and execute your projects with efficiency and flexibility.

What you will learn

In the following pages, you will discover how to:
*   Build a clear and inspiring vision of your goals
*   Identify your priorities and eliminate unnecessary distractions

- Use agile tools like sprints, backlogs, and retrospectives to make steady progress
- Stay motivated by balancing visualization and concrete action
- Handle unexpected events with agility, while staying on course

Who is this book for?

- For those who dream big but feel overwhelmed by the magnitude of their aspirations
- For perfectionists who want to structure their ideas without sacrificing their creativity
- For those who have tried the law of attraction but have struggled to move from intention to action
- For personal development enthusiasts seeking a concrete and balanced approach

A powerful synergy

The law of attraction helps you understand **why your goals** matter deeply to you. Scrum shows you how to achieve them, with clear and adaptable steps.

Together, these two approaches create a comprehensive method:
- You dream big, but act with method
- You cultivate a positive mindset, but you move step by step towards measurable results

- You become the project manager of your own life, capable of turning your most ambitious intentions into reality

A guide for pragmatic dreamers

This book is designed for those who want more than just a dose of inspiration or a list of tasks to complete. It is meant for those who seek a clear path to bring their dreams to life, without sacrificing the joy and serenity that come with a positive mindset.

It's not just about believing in your potential, but about structuring and organizing it so that it becomes an unstoppable force of achievement. By combining the power of your intentions with the discipline of a proven method, you're not just hoping: you are **creating, building, and accomplishing**.

How it all began

Ah, Christmas! That unique moment when we gather with family, sharing laughter, memories... and sometimes a few tense discussions. There's always Aunt Sylvie asking if you're still single and Uncle who launches into political rants. Yes, it's cliché, but admit it, it often happens.

As for me, the conversations inevitably revolved around the same topic for the past three years: my breakup with the mother of my children and the house we had bought together. Three years already, and nothing had changed. I still lived in that house, unable to move to the next step: buying out my ex-partner's share to become the full owner. I was stuck, frozen in this situation, unable to move forward.

And, like every Christmas, my family didn't fail to remind me of this stagnation. My sister-in-law and my brother, frustrated to see me in this situation, insisted: « Why haven't you sorted this out yet? What are you waiting for?»

It was in this context that, that evening, glass in hand, I found myself under the family spotlight. They had decided to film me, capturing the solemn promise that I would sort this out. « Next year, for sure, I'll do it! » I proclaimed with conviction, in a mix of pressure and hope.

But what to do, exactly? In recent months, I had spent a lot of time working on myself. My life was paced by my therapy sessions, which I had been attending for several months, and by heated discussions with my friends, including a personal development coach who introduced me to some of the concepts found in this book.

Still, I remained stuck, unable to take certain essential steps toward regaining total material freedom.

The house, entirely mine... It sounded like a deliverance, didn't it? But just the thought of starting this project overwhelmed me. The complex procedures, difficult decisions, and a colossal effort. Yet, it was a crucial goal. And around me, everyone was astonished that I was still stuck in stagnation.

«But move, Lionel! » Isa, a dear friend, my brother, my sister-in-law... they all reminded me that I couldn't keep going like this.

Yet, the path seemed full of obstacles. I had to make an appointment with a notary, contact my ex to discuss – not a pleasant prospect, given our strained relationship and near nonexistent communication. Then, there was the possibility of needing to hire a lawyer in case of disagreement, getting the house appraised, choosing one or more brokers, changing banks, closing joint accounts, redirecting my payments...
Even worse, I also had to consider handing over a sum with several zeros to my ex. All of this paralyzed me. It was a goal with heavy consequences, but it was also a necessary step to move forward.

Despite that, this breakup, against all odds, turned out to be beneficial in many ways. I had reconnected on a deeper level with my family.

What could be more enjoyable than spending hours chatting with loved ones? This strengthened bond gave me a new sense of momentum.

I had also embarked on a true journey of self-work. My bookshelf was overflowing with personal development books that I had devoured over the months. These readings had opened up new perspectives for me. I also worked with a personal development coach, whose insightful advice allowed me to explore transformative concepts: the law of attraction, NLP, EFT, the Karpman drama triangle, the dynamics of romantic relationships... I even sometimes traveled to Paris to attend workshops and meet several coaches who helped me evolve. Each discovery provided me with tools to better understand and shape my life.

My circle of friends had expanded. I now had reliable people around me, people I could count on. On the romantic front, even though my relationships were not always stable, they were exciting and fulfilled me in many ways. I attracted remarkable women, often beautiful and captivating. I had taken the time to write, with clarity and intention, my vision of the ideal partner. And, to my surprise, this vision seemed to be working !

I remember that specific moment when I imagined telling someone that I was in a relationship with a former model. That image, so vivid in my mind, soon became reality: I actually found myself talking to her about a beautiful woman, a former model, with whom I was having a relationship.

Indeed, at that moment, I had met a girl I had been talking to for months on Instagram. It turned out she was a perfect match for me—beautiful, intelligent, and she fit the clear vision I had defined for myself.

Later, I dated another girl for months who had also been a model. Just a coincidence? Was it a result of my concrete actions, my intentions, or some special aura?

In any case, these experiences proved to me the power of vision and intention. But they were not always without challenges. Some relationships lacked stability, and there were times when I felt discouraged. Still, this period allowed me to better understand what I truly wanted and refine my perception of myself and my aspirations.

I needed more discipline, more clarity, to finally live the life of my dreams. To free myself materially from my ex, to build a relationship with a woman I love, to explore the world by traveling to several countries... These aspirations still seemed out of reach.

But it was time to change. I decided to take control of my life, redefine my priorities and goals. And that's when an idea came to me. A simple but powerful idea. An idea that would shake up my perspective and transform my reality.

This revelation, this breakthrough, is what I'm going to share with you. Get ready, because it could very well change your life too!

That moment is etched in my memory. I had decided to give myself a break, a real pause to breathe and reconnect with myself. Shortly after that Christmas episode, at the very beginning of the year, I rented a small wooden cabin nestled in the Alps, above Albertville, far from the bustle of everyday life. Three days of complete tranquility, no cell phone. Just me, my books, a pen, and a notebook.

Like Bill Gates, I treated myself to a 'Think Week,' cut off from the rest of the world, to read and reflect. I desperately needed it, at a time when I felt completely drained.

Everything had come crashing down. My annual performance review had been a cold shower: I hadn't met my goals. At the same time, my ex—who clearly couldn't grasp the simplicity of a Lego-related matter—managed to insult me by text just before I left for this peaceful retreat. To top it all off, my love life was anything but stable. And of course, there was that infamous Christmas moment, just a few days earlier. I had found myself in front of my family, solemnly promising that I would finally buy out that damn house. Don't worry, I wasn't drunk! Christmas or not, I knew exactly what I was doing.

That weekend was a breath of fresh air. A pause to step away from the noise, reflect, write, and read freely. A chance to find some clarity amid the whirlwind of my life.

The place was breathtaking: a large sofa that doubled as a bed, minimalist wooden decor, wide bay windows offering a stunning view of the valley, and a skylight to gaze at the stars at night. All of it packed into just 30 square meters of simplicity and authenticity.

Disconnecting is sometimes all we need to make space for reflection. Far from social media, endless debates on Facebook, or the trivial comments of conspiracy theorists and boomers, far from Instagram and its filtered lives.

Cutting yourself off from the world is essential. Who wouldn't be drawn to the soothing calm of the mountains, the fresh air, and that breathtaking view? It gives me chills. Doesn't it do the same for you?

I started by taking stock of what wasn't working in my life, of what I absolutely wanted to improve, and I made a list of goals for the new year. Here's what I wrote down at the time, and I'm sharing it with you:

Buy out the house share
It had been three years since we separated, and yet the house we had bought together was still co-owned. It had become essential for me to become the sole owner, to sever the last material tie with my ex-partner. Of course, our children would always be the unbreakable bond between us, but this step symbolized my quest for freedom and reinvention.

Be in a relationship with an amazing woman
I've never stayed single for very long, but this time, I wanted to experience a stable relationship again. I met several

women, but nothing truly clicked. That year, I wanted to find the one with whom I could build something lasting.

Buy a hybrid car

My car was costing me a fortune in gas. You know the type—one of those big gas-guzzling SUVs eating up €400 a month in fuel and doing 8 liters per 100 km? Keeping such a beast wasn't part of my plan—especially one that emitted as much CO_2 as a herd of cows after a cassoulet buffet. Simplicity and sustainability are essential! Plus, I was dreaming of a sporty hybrid car with real power. Time to ditch the boring dad-mobile!

Take a great trip

The previous year, I had booked a camping trip with my kids. It was our first vacation together as a trio, and honestly, it wasn't a big success. So, on that day, I decided to treat them to a real trip, somewhere much more beautiful. It didn't have to be on the other side of the world—the goal was to enjoy our time together and find a vacation that would truly make us happy. Sometimes, the simplest goals are the best!

Take my place as a leader at work

For a while, I held a position at a startup, a place where it's great to work. But I had allowed myself to get trapped in a role too small for me. I was in a key position, yet I found myself doing secondary tasks, far from my true leadership role.

I wasn't stepping into my role, I wasn't the manager I was supposed to be. I made the decision to change everything, to embrace my role as a leader, and to fully take on my responsibilities.

These goals are choices to move forward, to no longer let life slip through my fingers. And you, what are your goals?

I had the idea that weekend to merge the law of attraction with the Scrum framework to achieve my dreams. I spent part of my free time reading personal development books, while my professional life was guided by the application of Scrum methodology. I had actually been trained in this methodology and obtained a certification a few years ago! And you know what? Combining a positive mindset with a proven agile methodology allowed me to better manage my life and finally see it improve! !

This is what I present to you in this book, which will help you achieve your goals just like I did!

Part 1: Creating a Powerful Vision

Before starting to run, it is essential to know where you're going. That's why creating a powerful vision is so important. When it's clear, inspiring, and deeply aligned with your desires, this vision becomes the foundation of everything you undertake. It acts as a compass, guiding you at every step, even when the path seems unclear or filled with obstacles.

In this first part, we will explore the importance of defining what we truly want, identifying our deepest aspirations, and building a vision that resonates with our whole being. We will learn how to transform our dreams into tangible reality by focusing our energy and actions on what truly matters to us. Whether you want to change careers, live a more fulfilled life, or simply accomplish a major project, a powerful vision is the key to getting started on the right foot.

Ready to map out your future with newfound clarity? Now is the time to define what you truly want, visualize your success, and ensure that every day brings you one step closer to that vision.

1 - Defining Your Goals

Clarifying What You Truly Desire

One of the first essential steps to manifesting your dreams into reality is to clarify what you truly desire. This is a crucial step, often overlooked, but it makes all the difference between aimless busyness and focused action that brings you closer to your deepest aspirations.

Becoming Aware of Your Deep Desires

It's easy to get swept up in superficial desires dictated by external forces: society, others, or even the pressures of daily life. But to use the law of attraction effectively, it's essential to connect with what you truly want, deep within yourself. Take the time to ask yourself the right questions:

- What truly makes me happy?
- If I could have anything I wanted, what would it be?
- What are the things that truly excite me, that motivate me, regardless of others' expectations?

Avoid focusing solely on material or external goals. It is your values, your passions, and your true aspirations that will guide you toward a fulfilling and aligned life.

During this weekend of introspection, I took the time to write down everything that, in my opinion, could truly enrich my life and bring me towards a more fulfilling reality. This vision was mine, unique, shaped by my aspirations at the time. What brings meaning and joy to one person may be completely different from what brings it to another. It's up to you to define what will make up your own ideal reality! Maybe it's opening a bakery, reconnecting with your family, or finally getting your motorcycle license to acquire the bike of your dreams.

Freeing yourself from external expectations

It's common for our desires to be influenced by what society expects of us. You may feel that you absolutely need to own a house, have a successful career, or constantly be on the move to succeed. Yet, these external expectations are not necessarily yours.

Learn to free yourself from these pressures by listening to your inner voice. Remember that every individual is unique, and what others consider to be a 'success' should not be your sole reference.

Some time ago, I came across a Facebook article about young people from rural backgrounds, leaving to study and build their careers in Paris. Future communication managers, lawyers, or even CEOs, some dream of great successes in the capital, while others wouldn't leave their hometown for anything, preferring to take over the family farm, surrounded by landscapes they hold dear.

In the comments, one sentence particularly struck me: « Burn out at 40 and have a Rolex at 50?» To which another user wisely replied, « The Rolex only tells the time, and lost time can't be bought. »

Taking Time for Introspection

To clarify what you truly desire, it's important to engage in honest introspection. You can take an entire weekend, like I do, away from the world; in my opinion, this is the ideal time —a key moment for effective introspection. Use this time to connect with yourself.

Meditate, write in a journal, and take solitary walks in nature. Sometimes, the mind needs calm to truly center itself and let your real desires emerge.

Write down your thoughts, ideas, and dreams. Don't censor them. Clarity will come with time. The more honest you are with yourself, the more you'll understand what you truly desire. You can repeat this exercise multiple times throughout the year whenever you feel the urge, but it's important to start with this step to begin this method.

Visualize your desires

Once you have become aware of your true desires, it's important to visualize them with precision. The law of attraction is based on the idea that what you focus your energy and attention on will manifest in your life. If your goals are vague or unclear, your energy will be scattered, and it will be difficult to manifest what you truly want.

Close your eyes and imagine yourself already living your goal. Feel the emotion associated with that moment. How do you feel? What is the atmosphere around you? The clearer and more vivid your vision is, the more you will attract concrete opportunities to make it happen.

Set clear and precise intentions

When you are clear about what you desire, you can now set precise intentions. An intention is more than just a wish. It's a commitment to yourself to bring that reality into being.

Phrase your intentions positively and in the present, as if what you desire is already happening. For example, instead of saying « I want to lose weight » say « I am in perfect health and take care of my body every day. » This affirmation puts you in the mindset of someone who is already taking action to achieve their dreams. For me, here are some positive affirmations I repeat: « I stay positive in all circumstances » «I push the company forward » Over time, these realities become deeply rooted within me, like a seed that sprouts in my mind.

Align your actions with your desires

Clarifying what you desire is an important step, but it's not enough.

You must also be ready to take concrete actions.
That's why I've linked positive affirmation with the Scrum methodology—it's this methodology that will enable you to take the necessary steps. With each move, you can check if your actions are aligned with your goals. Remember, every action, no matter how small, brings you closer to the reality you want to create.

Conclusion

Clarifying what you truly desire is laying the solid foundation on which you will build your success.

Once you have defined what you want with precision, you can focus your energy and use the law of attraction to bring what you desire into your life. But that's not enough: you'll also need aligned actions and an unwavering belief in your ability to transform your dreams into reality. Be clear in your intentions and make decisions that lead you toward the life you deserve.

Practical Exercise No. 1: Identify Your Aspirations

- First, take a sheet of paper and write down all the things you dream of accomplishing — anything that makes you feel good just thinking about it. It could be skydiving, changing jobs to become a winemaker, or visiting a new country
- Then, sort them by order of importance, from the one that brings the most value to your life to the least
- Finally, assign a color to each dream

Purpose of this exercise

The goal of this exercise is to clarify your deepest aspirations and give direction to your desires by organizing and visualizing them. By listing everything you dream of accomplishing, you connect with what inspires and motivates you, which can bring an immediate sense of joy and excitement.

By ranking these dreams in order of importance, you identify those that have the greatest impact on your well-being and personal fulfillment. This helps you prioritize and focus your energy on what truly matters to you.

Associating a color with each dream adds a visual and emotional dimension to the exercise. Colors can symbolize the intensity, nature, or emotion connected to each goal, making your aspirations even more vivid and tangible. This strengthens your commitment and stimulates your imagination to begin transforming those dreams into reality.

Activate the Law of Attraction: Align Yourself with Your Deepest Intentions

The Law of Attraction is a powerful principle: it is based on the idea that our thoughts, emotions, and actions determine what we attract into our lives. However, for it to truly work, it must be used intentionally and in alignment with your deepest desires. In this section, you will learn how to clarify your intentions, align your energy, and truly connect with your goals.

The Law of Attraction, Simply Explained

The Law of Attraction is based on a fundamental principle: what you focus your attention on manifests in your reality. Your thoughts, emotions, and beliefs act like magnets, attracting situations, people, and opportunities that match your vibration.

If you focus on what you truly desire with gratitude and confidence, you increase your chances of attracting it. Conversely, if you dwell on what you lack or on your fears, you may end up creating more of those negative experiences.

Clarify Your Intentions to Attract What Truly Matters

To use the Law of Attraction effectively, it is crucial to have a clear vision of your goals. Ask yourself the right questions to define your true intentions:

- What do you truly want in this phase of your life?
- Why is it important to you?
- How would you feel if you achieved this goal?

Take the time to write down your answers. Formulate your goals clearly, positively, and in the present tense. For example, instead of saying « I want less stress » say: « I live each day in serenity and balance. » This precision helps you focus your energy on what you want, not on what you want to avoid.

Feel before receiving: the power of emotion

The universe doesn't respond only to your thoughts, but also to the emotional energy you put into them. When you visualize your goals, imagine yourself already living them. Feel the joy, gratitude, and satisfaction associated with their achievement. These positive emotions strengthen your connection to your desires and increase your attracting power.

Practical tip: take five minutes each day to imagine yourself in the situation you wish to manifest. Live this moment in your mind as if it were already real. I try to do this every morning when I'm driving to work or at home before starting my day.

Harmonize your mind and actions to manifest with impact

The law of attraction works when your thoughts, beliefs, and actions are in harmony. If you have an ambitious goal but hold limiting beliefs such as « I'm not capable » or « I don't deserve it » you risk blocking the process.

Identify and replace these negative beliefs with positive affirmations. For example, if you doubt your ability to succeed, replace that thought with: « I am competent and capable of achieving my goals. »

Furthermore, your actions must reflect your intentions. For example, if your goal is to find a fulfilling job, start by updating your resume, actively applying, and expanding your network. Every small action strengthens the message you send to the universe

Cultivate Gratitude: The Subtle Fuel of Your Manifestations

Gratitude is one of the most powerful tools of the law of attraction. When you are grateful for what you already have, you raise your vibration and attract more abundance. Every day, take a moment to thank the universe, or simply yourself, for the opportunities and progress you've made. Even the smallest successes deserve to be celebrated. This practice helps you stay focused on the positive and maintain an open and receptive attitude.

Every evening, I take my notebook, write the date, and jot down three positive things that happened during my day. It strengthens me in my progress and successes each day. It's often easier to let our minds wander through the day and only focus on the things that bothered us – the colleague who spoke harshly to us, the friend who didn't answer the phone, the raise that still hasn't come. But by writing down and appreciating the positive moments of our day, our mindset improves, and it becomes more positive day after day.

Some time ago, I set myself a challenge: to take salsa and bachata classes with a friend. Yes, me, the king of stiffness, facing the swiveling hips and spinning turns.
Every other Friday, it's become our little ritual. We show up to class, more or less ready to follow what the instructor effortlessly demonstrates.

On my side? It's often a disaster festival. Between my hesitant steps and my free-styling arms, I look more like a disjointed puppet than a dancer. Tired after a workday, I sometimes only crave my couch, not a sequence of pasos dobles. And yet... I keep going.

Because despite everything, I enjoy myself. And above all, I progress. A little. Every session. And those little victories, I write them down. They strengthen my positive mindset. They remind me that every aligned action, even imperfect, nurtures my intention. And that's what matters.

Trust the process: sow today, reap tomorrow

Manifesting your goals may take time. Some aspirations require energetic alignment and circumstances that aren't immediate. Learn to trust the process. Keep nurturing your intentions with faith and perseverance, without getting discouraged by results that seem slow to arrive.

Remember: sometimes, what doesn't manifest right away is simply being prepared in the background. Be patient and stay open to unexpected opportunities.

Conclusion

Using the law of attraction to target your deep intentions and connect with your goals is a blend of introspection, visualization, and aligned actions.

Clarify what you truly desire, feel the positive emotions associated with your dreams with intensity, and act in alignment with your aspirations.

By integrating these principles into your daily life, you will become a true architect of your reality, capable of attracting and manifesting your deepest desires..

Practical Exercise No. 2: Write Down Your Gratitudes

- Every evening, write down three positive things from the day in a notebook

The goal of this exercise :

Writing down three positive things each day in a journal is a simple yet profoundly beneficial practice. It is based on principles of positive psychology and neuroscience, which show that our brain tends to focus on the negative as a protective mechanism. By writing down positive moments, even the smallest ones, you reprogram your mind to notice more of the pleasant aspects of your life. This habit helps you cultivate a more optimistic mindset and better manage difficult times.

Gratitude, which naturally flows from this practice, is a powerful lever for improving well-being. By identifying what is going well in your life, you develop a sense of appreciation for what you have, rather than focusing on what is missing. This contributes to better mental health, reduces stress, and fosters more fulfilling relationships. Recalling positive moments also activates neural circuits associated with happiness, thus strengthening your ability to see the good side of things, even on less favorable days.

Writing in a journal every day is also a way to give yourself a moment of calm and reflection. It allows you to slow down, reconnect with yourself, and bring a touch of mindfulness into your daily life. Over time, this journal becomes a valuable source of memories and motivation. Reading through your notes can revive moments of joy or remind you of your progress, which is particularly helpful during times of doubt or discouragement.

This routine can be easily incorporated into your daily life. Just a few minutes are enough, for example, before going to bed, to list three positive things: a smile exchanged, a task well done, an inspiring conversation, or a moment of relaxation. By adopting this habit, you create a virtuous circle that helps you appreciate each day more and build a more resilient and balanced mindset.

2 - Eliminate Mental Blockages

Identify and Overcome Limiting Beliefs

Our beliefs shape our reality. They influence the way we perceive the world, interpret events, and respond to challenges. Among them, some are enriching and motivating, while others hold us back: these are limiting beliefs.

These thoughts, often ingrained in us since childhood or formed by past experiences, can act like invisible barriers. They convince us that certain dreams are out of reach or that we are not "enough" – not competent enough, not lucky enough, not deserving enough.

Imagine an elephant tied to a simple stake. Since it was young, it was taught that it couldn't break free. As an adult, it has the strength to uproot it... but it doesn't even try. This is exactly what our limiting beliefs do.

Why identify your limiting beliefs?

It is impossible to overcome an obstacle that you do not recognize. Becoming aware of your limiting beliefs is the first step in deconstructing them. Without this awareness, they will continue to dictate your choices and hold back your ambitions, often unconsciously.

Common Examples of Limiting Beliefs

"I'm not smart enough to succeed."
A false belief that hinders learning and taking risks.

"I don't have enough time or money."
A belief that justifies inaction and limits opportunities.

"Others succeed because they're lucky, not me."
This diminishes your ability to recognize and seize your own opportunities.

"If I fail, it means I'm a failure."
A thought that ties your personal worth to your results, fueling the fear of trying anything.

How to Identify Your Limiting Beliefs

1. Take a pause and observe your thoughts.
When an idea or fear arises ("I can't do this"), take a moment to examine it. Is it based on facts or assumptions ?

2. Write down your blocks.
Grab a notebook and jot down the situations where you feel stuck. What thoughts come up frequently ?

3. Ask yourself key questions.
- What is the origin of this belief ?
- Is it really true, or just an interpretation ?
- How does this thought influence my actions or decisions ?

Deconstructing Your Limiting Beliefs

Once you've identified your beliefs, it's time to challenge them and replace them with empowering thoughts.

1. Bring in contrary evidence.

Look for examples where this belief didn't hold true. For instance, if you think « I'm never lucky » recall a time when you succeeded through your own efforts.

2. Reframe the belief.
Turn a limiting thought into a positive and empowering affirmation. For example :
- **Limiting belief :** *"I'm not competent enough."*
- **New belief :** *"I am capable of learning and improving over time."*

3. Adopt a new perspective.
Imagine what a close friend or mentor would say in your place. Their supportive outlook can help you see things from a different angle

Practice Regularly to Unlock Your Potential

Changing limiting beliefs takes time and consistency. Here are a few simple practices to help reinforce your new empowering thoughts :

- **Visualization :** Picture yourself succeeding in situations where you previously felt stuck.
- **Positive Affirmations :** Repeat empowering phrases daily to reprogram your mindset.

- **Reflection :** Each evening, write down a success or small win to show your brain that you are making progress.

A Life Freed from Limiting Beliefs

By identifying and overcoming your limiting beliefs, you open yourself to new opportunities and perspectives. This process is not just a step toward achieving your goals—it is a profound transformation that allows you to see your abilities in a new light. When you release these invisible burdens, a world of possibilities unfolds. You begin to realize that you are not only capable, but also deserving of everything you aspire to accomplish.

Practical Exercise No. 3: Replace Your Limiting Beliefs

1- Identify Your Limiting Beliefs :
- Reflect on a situation where you felt stuck or unable to take action
- Write down the thoughts that came to your mind in that moment. For example: « I'm not competent enough » « I don't have the time » « Others are more successful than I am. »
- Ask yourself: What negative phrase do I often repeat to myself ?

2 - Analyze Their Origin :
For each limiting belief you've identified, ask yourself :

- Where does this belief come from? (A past experience, something someone close to you said, an inner fear...)
- Is this belief based on a fact or merely a perception ?

3 - Challenge These Beliefs :
Take each belief and ask yourself :
- Is this true 100% of the time ?
- Do I have concrete evidence to support this idea ?
- Are there examples that show the opposite ?

For example, if you believe « I'm not creative» recall a time when you had an original idea or created something creative

4 - Replace them with positive and empowering beliefs :
Reframe each limiting belief into a positive affirmation. For example :
- *"I'm not competent enough" becomes "I am learning and improving every day"*
- *"I don't have time" becomes "I can prioritize and make time for what matters"*

5 - Take action to reinforce the new belief :
Identify a small, concrete action you can take right away to validate your new belief.
For example, if your new belief is "I am creative," you might decide to draw something or share a new idea during a meeting.

6 - Repeat and visualize :
Each day, reread your new positive beliefs and visualize yourself living them.

Imagine the results you could achieve by acting according to these new ideas

7 - **Measure your progress :**
Regularly note the situations where you acted differently thanks to your new belief.
This will boost your self-confidence and strengthen this transformation

Purpose of this exercise

This exercise will not only help you become aware of the thoughts that hold you back but also replace them with beliefs that drive you toward your goals.

Visualization and Focus: Activate the Power of Your Mind

Visualizing and focusing are two powerful tools to turn your dreams into reality. It's not magic, but a mental exercise that directs your energy toward what truly matters.
Here's how these techniques work and how to integrate them into your daily life.

What is Visualization ?

Visualization is the practice of using your imagination to create a clear and detailed mental image of what you want to achieve. It's a way of "living" your goals in advance, making them tangible in your mind before they become reality. The idea is simple: the more clearly and intensely you focus on a goal, the more you align your thoughts, emotions, and actions toward its achievement.

Why does visualization work ?

Our brain reacts almost the same way to a vividly imagined situation as it does to a real experience. Visualization is training your mind to succeed even before taking action. When you visualize with precision, you activate the same brain areas as if you were actually living the situation. This strengthens your confidence, boosts your motivation, and prepares your mind to seize the opportunities that come your way.

Create a vivid, sensory, and emotional visualization.

Visualization becomes more powerful the more alive it feels. Imagine your goal in detail: the places, colors, sounds. Engage all five senses to make the mental image more real. If you dream of a house, visualize the texture of the walls, the smell of wood or nature around, the light streaming through the windows. If you aspire to an inspiring career, imagine the office atmosphere, positive interactions, shared successes.

But don't stop at the images. Feel the emotions that come with this achievement: joy, pride, freedom, gratitude. These emotions are the invisible fuel that transforms a mental image into a lasting source of motivation

Practice daily.

Set aside 5 to 10 minutes each day to visualize your goals. Do this in a quiet place where you can fully concentrate without interruptions.

The Power of Concentration

Concentration is essential to support visualization. It's not enough to just dream—you need to focus your attention on the actions required to turn your visions into reality.

1. Set a Clear Intention.

CStart each day by defining a specific intention related to your goal. For example: « Today, I will take a step forward in building my business »

2. Avoid Distractions.

Today, our environment is flooded with distractions: constant notifications, digital interruptions, and nonstop multitasking. According to a study from the University of California, it takes an average of **23 minutes** to regain focus after being interrupted. It's no surprise that productivity and mental clarity suffer as a result.

For a long time, I was trapped in this digital trap myself. From the moment I woke up, I checked my phone, switching from one app to another — Instagram, emails, news... The result was a constant mental fog and the feeling that my day had slipped away without really starting.

Everything changed the day I realized that my focus was my most precious asset. I turned off notifications, adopted a "focus mode," and structured my days into time blocks. Within weeks, my productivity soared. But more importantly, I reconnected with what truly matters.
Focus isn't regained by chance: it must be protected and cultivated. And it will transform your daily life.

3. Use focusing tools.

◦ **Breathing techniques**: Take a few moments to breathe deeply and calm your mind before concentrating.

∘ **Guided meditation**: Use apps or videos to train your mind to focus on a single thought or image.
∘ **Priority list**: Write down the three most important tasks of the day and focus only on them.

Combining Visualization and Focus

The magic happens when you use these two tools together. Here's how :

1. Visualize your goals to boost motivation and clarify your vision.
2. Focus on specific actions to turn that vision into reality.

For example, if you dream of running a marathon, start by visualizing the finish line, the cheering crowd, and the feeling of accomplishment. Then, focus on your daily training plan— one step at a time.

Conclusion

With regular practice of visualization and focus, you'll begin to notice tangible changes in your life :
• Your goals will become clearer.
• You'll feel more motivated to take action.
• You'll start recognizing and seizing opportunities that bring you closer to your aspirations.

Visualization + Focus = Transformation.
By combining mental clarity with purposeful action, you move from dreaming to achieving.

Practical Exercise No. 4: Meditate !

Practice one guided meditation per week

Guided meditation is a powerful tool to calm the mind, refocus, and reconnect with your goals — especially when daily life feels overwhelming.

Whenever I feel the need, I take the time to practice a mindfulness meditation. These moments, simple yet profound, help me return to what truly matters: my energy, my sensations, the present moment.

It's a deliberate pause amid the chaos — a return to myself.

How to do it ?

1 - Schedule a fixed time: Choose a weekly time slot, such as Sunday evening or Monday morning.

2 - Find a meditation: Use apps (like Headspace, Insight Timer) or YouTube videos that suit your needs

3- Create a calm atmosphere: Settle into a peaceful space, dim the lights, and sit comfortably

4- Listen and let yourself be guided: Simply follow the voice and allow your mind to relax

Purpose of this exercise :

The goal of this exercise is to help you calm your mind, reconnect with yourself, and gain clarity on your goals.
By practicing guided meditation regularly, you create mental space to refocus, reduce stress, and strengthen your inner motivation.
It's a powerful way to recharge and realign your actions with your true aspirations

Part 2: The Power of Positive Intention

A clear vision is essential, but without a positive intention to support it, it may remain just an idea—a vague aspiration. Intention is the invisible engine, the energy that brings your dreams to life. It transforms your thoughts into actions, and your actions into results. In this section, we'll explore how to harness the power of your intention to attract what you truly desire into your life.

Positive intention goes far beyond just having a constructive mindset. It's an active force—a deep conviction that what you want is not only possible, but already unfolding. By cultivating this intention, you align yourself with your aspirations, and this is how you begin to attract opportunities, resources, and people who will help you achieve your goals.

By focusing on what you want—rather than on what you don't—you begin to reshape your reality. It's a true shift in perspective, and you're about to learn how to use it to turn every moment of your life into a step toward success. Ready to unlock the power of intention? Now is the time to leap forward—with confidence and clarity—toward the life you've always envisioned.

1 - Thoughts shape reality

How Your Thoughts Influence Your Life Experience

Our thoughts are far more powerful than we imagine. They don't just drift through our minds like clouds in the sky—they actively shape our reality. What you think about repeatedly influences how you perceive the world, the choices you make, and ultimately, the life you live.

I don't know exactly how it happened, but it did. Shortly after my breakup, a clear image came to me: I saw myself sitting on a white leather sofa, in a familiar place, telling someone about my new life, my projects, my encounters. The scene felt both ordinary and significant, almost prophetic. I would visualize it regularly, with a particular intensity. Let me share a personal experience that illustrates the power of thought. A few months later, I met Coralie on an app. It was love at first sight. On our first date, she told me she had been a model and had won a competition—a striking detail that seemed strangely familiar.

One day, while telling a friend from my past life about this encounter, I realized that the scene I had imagined had manifested almost exactly as I had envisioned it. As if the repeated visualization had paved the way for it to become reality. My thought, anchored in the present, had ultimately shaped the future.

And it wasn't an isolated case. On several occasions, I noticed that my thoughts and intentions—when given consistent and sincere attention—had a direct impact on my life. Little by little, by focusing on my goals, my reality began to transform.

Your thoughts shape your beliefs

What you think regularly becomes your truth.

• **Recurring thought**: « I'm not good at this»
Over time, this thought takes root, and you end up genuinely believing you're incapable.

• **Positive thought**: « I'm learning at every step »
It becomes an empowering belief that drives you to take action despite challenges.

Your thoughts create the framework through which you interpret the world. This framework influences what you notice, what you overlook, and how you respond to events.

Your beliefs dictate your actions

A strong belief becomes the filter through which you make your decisions. If you believe you don't deserve success, you may miss opportunities. Conversely, if you are convinced that you can achieve your goals, you will put in the necessary effort to succeed, even in the face of obstacles !

Your actions are therefore a direct reflection of your deepest thoughts. By adopting a positive and determined mindset, you naturally steer your behaviors toward success.

Your actions transform your reality

Every thought leads to an action, and every action helps build your life.

• **Negative thought:** « I don't have time to improve »
Result: You make no changes to your daily routine.

• **Positive thought:** « I will dedicate 15 minutes a day to progress »
Result: You create a new habit that, over time, changes your reality.

Even the smallest actions, repeated consistently, can have a huge impact. And it all starts with a simple thought. Honestly, I could have made excuses a thousand times: "I don't have time," "It's too complicated," all the usual excuses. But each time, I held on to positive thoughts and a clear visualization of my goals. Those small, consistent actions eventually build something big.

Let me give you a concrete example: early 2020, right in the middle of Covid, during the first lockdown. One morning, I stepped on the scale. That day was a shock. I looked at myself in the mirror: 65 kg for 1.85 m. Yes, 65 kg. I looked like a shrimp that escaped from a fishing net! Let's just say it was an electric shock. That day, I made a radical decision: I decided to sculpt my body.

Problem was, all the gyms were closed. But it didn't matter—I was determined. I started visualizing myself with muscles like the guys you see in magazines. No gimmicks, no exaggerated poses. This vision became my driving force. So, I researched exercises you could do at home, heard about a method that worked well, ordered some whey protein (because, of course, that's the basics), and built a solid routine. Day after day, I stuck to it like a zen monk of weightlifting—discipline and rigor every single day, without exception.

The result? In a few months, I gained between 12 and 15 kilos, mostly muscle. When the lockdown ended, I reunited with my family, and some of them were totally shocked. I still remember their incredulous looks. That moment was a victory. Thanks to my clear vision and solid routine, I managed to reach one of my goals from the past few years. And you know what? Since then, I've even posed for several photographers. No, I'm not in fitness magazines yet, but I did model for a men's underwear brand. Yes, me—the shrimp from before. It just goes to show: a clear vision and consistency can truly transform a life... and a body!

The Effect of Neuroplasticity: When Your Thoughts Reprogram Your Brain

Your brain is malleable. What you think regularly strengthens certain neural circuits, a phenomenon called neuroplasticity.

- Negative thoughts reinforce connections related to stress and anxiety.
- Positive thoughts promote areas of the brain associated with creativity, resilience, and problem-solving.

By consciously choosing thoughts that uplift you, you literally train your brain to see opportunities instead of obstacles.

Techniques to Influence Your Thoughts

1. Identify your thought patterns.
Become aware of recurring negative or limiting thoughts.

2. Replace them with positive affirmations.
Transform a thought like « I'm not good enough » into « I improve every day»

3. Practice gratitude.
Focus on what you already have. Being grateful directs your mind toward abundance rather than scarcity.

4. Visualize your success.
Regularly imagine the life you want to create, as if it already exists. This conditions your mind to find ways to make it happen.

Concrete Examples

. At work: A negative thought like « I will never get that promotion » makes you less invested. A positive thought like

« I will prepare and give my best » motivates you to take action and increases your chances of success.

• **In relationships:** If you believe others don't like you, you may isolate yourself. Conversely, believing that you have a lot to offer opens you up to others and helps create meaningful connections.

Your Thoughts, an Immense Power

Each thought is a seed you plant in your mind. If you plant positive and motivating thoughts, you will harvest a life aligned with your aspirations.

If you let negative thoughts dominate, they will limit your potential. The good news is that you have the power to choose what you think. So, take a moment to reflect: :

Today, plant a thought. Tomorrow, harvest your new reality

The Importance of Cultivating a Positive Mindset

Your mindset is the key that opens the door to success, happiness, and fulfillment. It determines how you respond to events, how you face challenges, and, most importantly, how you perceive the world around you. A positive mindset is not just a surface attitude; it is an inner strength that guides your actions and transforms your reality.

Mindset: The Foundation of All Change

Your mindset is the foundation upon which every aspect of your life rests. It acts as a filter through which you view the world. A person with a positive attitude tends to see opportunities in challenges, while someone with a negative mindset might focus only on obstacles. It is not what happens in your life that determines your happiness, but rather how you respond to what happens.

Why is this so important ?

A positive mindset allows you to :

- **See possibilities**, even in difficult times.
- **Face challenges** with a constructive attitude.
- **Find solutions** instead of dwelling on problems.

When you cultivate a positive mindset, you remain in a constant state of readiness to receive the best, to learn, and to grow.

You stop letting the fear of failure paralyze you, and start seeing every situation as an opportunity for growth.

The Snowball Effect: Positive Thoughts to Transform Your Reality

When you deliberately choose to cultivate a positive mindset, you set off a snowball effect. You begin to see the bright side of things, and gradually, this influences your behavior and actions. For example, if you believe you can succeed, you will act with confidence and perseverance. This attitude shows up in your choices, interactions, and even your physical well-being.

A positive mindset not only influences how you act but also how others perceive you. Positive people attract other positive people. They build stronger relationships and surround themselves with opportunities because their energy is contagious.

The Link Between Mindset and Success

Many studies have shown that those who cultivate an optimistic attitude are more likely to succeed in various areas of their lives. This doesn't mean everything will magically fall into place, but a positive mindset helps you to :

- **Stay motivated** when facing obstacles.
- **Be more creative** in finding solutions to your problems.
- **Develop resilience** while going through difficult times.

One of the keys to success is maintaining the right attitude, even when things don't go as planned. People who give up easily tend to have a negative mindset. Those who succeed are the ones who, despite challenges, persevere with a positive attitude and a deep belief that they will eventually achieve their goals.

Cultivating a Positive Mindset Daily

The good news is that a positive mindset doesn't depend on external circumstances. It can be cultivated anytime, in any situation. Here are some simple practices to strengthen a positive mindset every day :

- **Gratitude:** Take a moment each day to reflect on what you're grateful for. This helps refocus your mind on the positive, even during difficult times.
- **Positive affirmations:** Speak kind and encouraging words to yourself. « I am capable of achieving my dreams » « Every day, I become a better version of myself.».
- **Letting go:** Learn to accept what cannot be changed and focus on what you can control. This prevents you from wasting energy dwelling on things beyond your reach.
- **Self-compassion:** Be kind to yourself, especially during moments of failure. Learn to forgive yourself and get back up, rather than criticizing yourself.

The impact of mindset on your physical and emotional well-being

Did you know that your mindset can also have a direct effect on your physical health? Studies show that optimistic people have stronger immune systems, experience less stress, and suffer less from chronic illnesses. This is explained by the effect of positive thoughts and emotions on the body, which reduce stress and promote better mental health.

Moreover, a positive mindset contributes to better emotional regulation. By developing the habit of thinking positively, you reduce feelings of frustration, anger, and sadness. You become better equipped to handle stressful situations without being overwhelmed by negative emotions.

A Positive Mindset as a Driver of Transformation

A positive mindset is not just about managing your attitude; it becomes a powerful driver of transformation. When you believe that you can change and that you are capable of creating the life you desire, you activate your inner potential. Every positive thought is a small seed that, over time, will grow into a tree of success, happiness, and well-being.

By cultivating a positive mindset, you allow yourself to attract the best into your life and to realize your deepest dreams. It is a form of self-empowerment, a daily choice that gradually transforms not only how you perceive your life but also how it manifests.

Conclusion

Cultivating a positive mindset is not a naive or unrealistic attitude. It is a powerful choice that allows you to navigate life with resilience, confidence, and hope. By changing the way you perceive the world, you directly influence the outcomes you achieve.

Never forget that your mindset is one of the key factors shaping your life experience. It's time to take that key and open the door to your future.

2 - Aligning Your Emotions with Your Goals

The Impact of Emotions on Attracting What You Want

Emotions are powerful signals, indicators that not only influence our well-being but also the way we interact with the world. They are, in fact, one of the most influential forces in the process of attraction— a key element to realizing your desires and transforming your life. Understanding and mastering the impact of your emotions can play an essential role in the success of your journey toward achieving your goals.

Emotions: a magnetism that attracts what you feel

The law of attraction is based on the idea that our thoughts, beliefs, and emotions emit a vibration that attracts similar situations, people, and opportunities into our lives.
This vibration is not simply the product of what we think but also of what we deeply feel.

Emotions are energies that flow through our being. When we experience positive emotions such as joy, love, gratitude, or enthusiasm, our vibrational frequency rises, and we become magnets for positive experiences. Conversely, negative emotions like anger, fear, sadness, or doubt lower our vibrational frequency and can attract experiences or situations that reinforce these feelings.

Why does this happen ?

The universe responds to how we feel, rather than to what we think.

Our emotions carry a very clear message to the universe: "This is what I want." This translates into attracting situations and opportunities that match the intensity and nature of our emotions. For example, if you are at peace with yourself, your mind emits a calm and positive energy, drawing to you circumstances that reinforce this state of tranquility.

The role of gratitude: an emotion that transforms

One of the most powerful ways to change the direction of your life is to cultivate a feeling of gratitude. When you feel grateful, you connect to a high frequency and emit positive vibrations. This emotion allows you to focus on what you already have, rather than what you lack. By being thankful for the small things in daily life, you send a powerful message to the universe that you are ready to receive more of these blessings.

Positive emotions vs. negative emotions: what differences in attraction?

Positive emotions have a direct attracting effect. They are like open doors that allow positive energy to flow freely into your life. Enthusiasm, confidence, and joy are states that naturally attract more pleasant situations. By focusing on these emotions, you create space for abundance and success.

On the other hand, negative emotions, although inevitable, can create energetic blockages. Fear, doubt, or anxiety, for example, tend to push away what you desire.

They distance you from your goal because they emit vibrations that are not aligned with what you truly want to attract. The more you focus on your fears or lacks, the more you attract them.

This doesn't mean you should ignore or repress your negative emotions. Accept them, understand them, but don't let them dominate your life. Transform them into a source of motivation, a call to action, or use them as a way to strengthen your desire for change.

Emotion: the key to manifested intention

It is not enough to simply set positive intentions. You must accompany them with powerful and sincere emotions for them to truly manifest in your life. The law of attraction does not merely draw what you desire on an intellectual level; it responds to the emotional intensity you attach to it.
When you deeply connect with what you want—whether it's a new career, a fulfilling relationship, or a more peaceful lifestyle—you need to genuinely feel those emotions. You must not only visualize your goal but also experience the joy and excitement of having already achieved it.

How to transform negative emotions into a driving force for change

It is normal to experience negative emotions, especially when facing life's challenges.

However, you have the power to transform these emotions into fuel to move forward toward your goals. The key is to acknowledge them and use them as leverage to take action.

Here are some strategies to transform negative emotions:

- **Take a step back:** Breathe deeply and observe the emotion without judgment. Accept it for what it is, without letting it define your state of mind..

- **Analyze the source:** Ask yourself where this emotion is coming from and what it is trying to teach you. It may be a signal indicating that something needs to change in your life.

- **Refocus your thoughts:** Notice when your mind drifts into negative thinking. Replace those thoughts with positive affirmations or mental images of what you truly want to attract.

The Power of Emotion Aligned with Action

When you combine positive emotions with concrete actions, you strengthen the effectiveness of the law of attraction. Emotion gives power to action, and action gives direction to emotion. This marriage between emotion and action is what makes manifestation possible.

Imagine you want to start a business. If you feel excitement, confidence, and passion for this project, and you act with conviction and determination, you send clear signals to the universe that you are ready to receive success.

The universe will respond to your enthusiasm by bringing you opportunities, ideas, and connections aligned with your mindset.

Conclusion

Emotions are powerful instruments that shape our reality. By cultivating positive emotions and pairing them with concrete actions, you can attract everything you desire. It is in this fusion of thoughts, feelings, and actions that the true power of the law of attraction lies. Be mindful of your emotions, guide them wisely, and you will see your life transform, driven by the energy you choose to manifest.

Techniques to Maintain Emotional Alignment with Your Aspirations

Emotional alignment is a key element in attracting what you desire in life. Your emotions act like an internal GPS, guiding your thoughts, actions, and outcomes. When you are aligned with your aspirations, you are in harmony with the energy you want to manifest. Conversely, when your emotions are out of balance, they can hinder your progress. Maintaining this alignment is therefore essential to turning your dreams into reality.

Here are some proven techniques to help you stay emotionally aligned with your goals.

Practice Mindfulness

Mindfulness is the art of being fully present in the moment, without judgment. It allows you to become aware of your emotions as they arise. Sometimes, we act impulsively or react without thinking, but mindfulness helps you stay centered and prevents you from being overwhelmed by negative emotions.

I must admit, I'm not usually one for sitting meditation sessions, but after trying mindfulness, I find it surprisingly calming — especially when I practice it with my son, who really enjoys these moments.

How to Practice ?

- Take a few minutes each day to focus on your breathing. Close your eyes and let your thoughts drift away.
- Observe your emotions without trying to change them. For example, if you feel anxious about your project, simply acknowledge it and let it pass without judgment.
- This practice helps you identify your emotional patterns and respond more consciously, adjusting your thoughts and actions to stay aligned with your aspirations.

Visualize Your Goals with Emotion

Visualization is a powerful technique to align your emotions with your goals. It's not just about imagining what you want, but also feeling the emotions that come with achieving those desires. The law of attraction works best when you pair positive emotions with your vision.

How to Visualize Effectively ?

- Take a few minutes each day to close your eyes and imagine that you have already achieved your goals.
- Feel the emotions tied to this success: pride, joy, gratitude, excitement.
- The more you feel these emotions, the clearer signals you send to the universe that you are ready to receive what you desire. This practice strengthens the alignment between your emotional state and your aspirations.

Positive Affirmations to Strengthen Your Mindset

Affirmations are positive statements that you repeat regularly to reprogram your subconscious and steer your emotions in a positive direction. They help build self-confidence and maintain a positive attitude, even in the face of challenges..

Examples of affirmations for emotional alignment :

- *"I am worthy of receiving everything I desire."*
- *"I am in perfect harmony with my aspirations."*
- *"Every day, I move closer and closer to my dreams. »*

How to use them ?

• Repeat your affirmations first thing in the morning to start your day on a positive note.
• Use them during moments of doubt or frustration to realign your emotions with your aspirations.
• Write them down in a journal or place them somewhere you can see them regularly. This way, they become a constant reminder of your goals and the positive energy you want to manifest.

Create a Vision Board

A vision board is a collage of images, words, and phrases that represent your goals and aspirations. Seeing your goals visually every day helps you stay focused and maintain an emotional alignment with what you want to attract into your life.

How to create a vision board ?

- Find a large sheet, board, or panel.
- Collect images, quotes, and objects that symbolize your goals. For example, if you want to start your own business, include images of entrepreneurial success, logos, or inspiring quotes.
- Place it somewhere you'll see it regularly, preferably every day. When you look at it, feel the satisfaction of having already achieved those goals. This will strengthen the alignment of your emotions with your aspirations.

A few years ago, I found myself sitting around a coffee table discussing the law of attraction with some acquaintances. I still remember this girl proudly holding up an A3 sheet filled with inspiring phrases and images that motivated her.

That very evening, I went home and decided to create my own! I immediately started searching for photos that inspired me or represented what I wanted in my life. A Finnish flag (that country has always fascinated me), money, the car of my dreams, smiling children's faces, a peaceful nature spot, a beautiful woman... In short, I put everything that made me dream on my board, ready to attract it all into my life!

Stay flexible and open to opportunities

One of the greatest challenges to inner harmony is not being too rigid or attached to a single way of achieving your dreams. Life often has surprising ways of leading you where you want to go, sometimes through unexpected paths.

Staying flexible allows you to maintain a positive attitude and seize opportunities that come your way, even if they don't exactly match what you imagined.

How to stay flexible ?

- Be ready to adapt your plans and change direction if necessary.
- Don't see failures or obstacles as permanent setbacks, but as opportunities to readjust your approach.
- Cultivate the trust that, no matter which path you take, you are always moving toward your aspirations.

The Importance of Self-Compassion

When working toward your goals, you will inevitably face moments of doubt, frustration, or fatigue. It is essential not to judge yourself too harshly. The key to maintaining emotional alignment is to treat every step of your journey with kindness and understanding.

How to Practice Self-Compassion ?

- Speak to yourself as you would to a close friend: with encouragement and kindness.
- If you make a mistake or encounter an obstacle, don't be too hard on yourself. Remember that every difficulty is an opportunity to learn.
- Take care of yourself, not only physically but also emotionally. Allow yourself breaks and moments of relaxation to recharge and maintain a healthy emotional state.

Conclusion

Maintaining emotional alignment with your aspirations is an ongoing process that requires attention and practice. The techniques we've discussed—mindfulness, visualization, affirmations, vision boards, flexibility, and self-compassion—are powerful tools to strengthen your emotional connection to your goals.

Remember that your emotions are valuable indicators. If you learn to understand and direct them toward your desires, you will create a powerful, coherent energy that guides you toward achieving your dreams. Emotional harmony is the key to unlocking your potential and manifesting a life that truly reflects who you are.

Practical Exercise No. 5: Create Your Vision Board

A Vision Board is not just a collage of inspiring images. It's a visual projection of your future, a daily reminder of what you want to accomplish. It helps you give clear direction to your thoughts and transform your desires into reality.

Start by reflecting on what you truly want. Imagine yourself one year, three years, five years from now. Where do you live? With whom? What do you do every day? Write these answers down in a journal, being as precise as possible. Note goals in different areas: career, health, travel, relationships, lifestyle...

Once your vision is clear, look for images, words, and quotes that represent it. Flip through magazines, print photos, cut out phrases that resonate with you. Assemble them on a corkboard, a large sheet, or a digital platform. Arrange them so the whole inspires you instantly.

Hang your Vision Board somewhere visible and make it a habit to look at it every day. Let these images soak into you, feel them as if they were already part of your life. But above all, take action. A dream becomes reality when you move toward it, even in small steps.

For my part, some time ago, I left my Vision Board hanging in my bedroom for a long while. I had put together several inspiring photos — a beautiful girl, happy children, the Finnish flag, the car I wanted, a peaceful nature spot... Now all that's left is to create yours!

Part 3: Scrum for Personal Life

Scrum Methodology, widely used by agile teams to manage complex projects, might seem far removed from our personal daily lives. Yet, its principles can completely transform the way you approach your life goals. In this part, we will explore how to adapt this powerful framework to your personal development, helping you achieve your dreams with renewed effectiveness.

Imagine being able to organize your goals the same way you would manage a professional project—but with total flexibility to follow your aspirations.

Scrum allows you to break down your big goals into concrete actions, track your progress regularly, and adjust your strategy according to the challenges you encounter.

This process offers you a structure while giving you the freedom to adjust your priorities based on your current needs and dreams—whether you're pursuing a career goal, nurturing a passion, or making personal changes.

Scrum is built on a few core principles: working in short cycles called sprints, setting clear and regular goals, and conducting retrospectives to make ongoing improvements. In the next chapter, we'll explain exactly what these terms mean and how you can apply them to your life. But for now, think of them simply as tools to help you structure your progress and stay flexible in the face of the unexpected.

Ready to take control of your life with a strategic and agile approach? It's time to bring Scrum into your daily routine! !

Scrum in Action: True Stories of Remarkable Success

Before diving into the practical application of the methodology, let's first look at some success stories from companies that have embraced Scrum.

Scrum is not just a framework reserved for developers tucked away in open-plan offices. It's a true catalyst for change, an accelerator of results, a revealer of talent. From Silicon Valley to Dutch classrooms, from banking towers to creative marketing studios, Scrum has proven its ability to transform not only projects—but lives.

Let me take you through a few stories—sometimes surprising, often inspiring—where Scrum truly made a difference.

Spotify: Harmony in Chaos

When thinking of agile success stories, Spotify is one of the first names that comes to mind. During a period of rapid growth, the streaming platform had to maintain constant innovation while staying organized.

They implemented squads—small, autonomous teams—each operating like a startup within the startup. Inspired by Scrum, these teams worked in sprints, with regular reviews and retrospectives.

One now-legendary anecdote: during a single sprint, a team completely reinvented the way playlists are recommended—in just two weeks. What started as a simple test turned into a massive success: listening rates skyrocketed. To this day, that algorithm remains a cornerstone of Spotify's success.

ING Bank: The Bank That Outpaced the Fintechs

CHow can a legacy bank compete with the agile startups shaking up the financial world? Dutch giant ING rose to the challenge by completely transforming its organization using Scrum principles.

They formed cross-functional teams bringing together developers, product managers, and business stakeholders. The result? A 60% reduction in delivery time. But that's not all.

A quick anecdote: During the very first sprint of a "consumer credit" team, they discovered that users were abandoning the application form on page 3. The team decided to immediately test a simplified version—and within two weeks, they had doubled the completion rate.

A Primary School in the Netherlands: Post-its and Children

Scrum in a primary school? Yes, you read that right.
A Dutch teacher decided to experiment with the framework
with her 10-year-old students. Every morning, they held a
Daily Meeting, set their weekly goals, and used a physical
board to visualize their progress.

The best part?
During a science project sprint, a group of children used
their sprint points to persuade the teacher to add a field trip.
They had prepared a retrospective with rock-solid
arguments.
The result: a visit to the science museum—approved by the
Product Owner (the teacher, of course!).

USA Today: The scoop before anyone else

Even newspapers are getting on board.
The American daily USA Today has adopted Scrum for its
digital newsroom. Each squad includes journalists, editors,
and developers. Together, they produce content in sprints,
adapting priorities as news evolves.

During a breaking news story, one team used a retrospective
to improve how journalists passed information to
developers. The result? An automated tagging system was
implemented in just one day—leading to faster coverage than
CNN on a major political event.

The Red Cross: Saving Lives with Post-it

When we think of "Scrum," we rarely picture humanitarian
crises.

Yet the Red Cross has used Scrum to improve the efficiency of some of its field operations—particularly during natural disasters.

Multidisciplinary teams composed of logisticians, doctors, coordinators, and volunteers were trained to work in very short sprints, often just 2 to 3 days, with daily meetings held directly on the ground—literally around the intervention map.
The backlog? A list of urgent actions, prioritized by humanitarian need: water, food, medical care, shelter.

A striking story:
During a post-earthquake mission in Southeast Asia, one Scrum team decided—after its retrospective—to entrust the distribution of survival kits to a local duo.
The result? Deliveries jumped from 100 to 600 families per day... simply because locals knew the usable roads better than any GPS.

From startups to schools, banks to media outlets, Scrum has emerged as a powerful tool for deep transformation.
Not just to ship code—but to create, learn, adapt, and improve.

The ingredients for success are all there :

- Clear, iterative goals,
- Regular feedback,
- Team autonomy,
- And most importantly... a culture that embraces trying, failing, adjusting, and growing.

Scrum doesn't just transform business projects.
It has the potential to transform your life—giving you direction and helping you move forward, even when life throws curveballs.
At every step, you'll progress, learn, and grow..

1 - Using Scrum to Achieve Your Goals

Introduction to Scrum Principles (Backlog, Sprint, Retrospectives)

Scrum is an agile methodology, often used by teams developing complex projects, but its effectiveness is not limited to the professional environment.

Indeed, it is a set of principles and practices that can be very relevantly applied to personal project management—whether for big life aspirations or simple short-term goals. This approach helps you structure and organize the achievement of your dreams and projects efficiently while remaining flexible in the face of obstacles and unexpected events.

To get started well, it is essential to understand three fundamental elements of Scrum: the **Backlog**, the **Sprints**, and the **Retrospectives**. These three tools are designed to help you turn your dreams into concrete, measurable, and achievable actions.

1. The Backlog: Your List of Goals

The **Backlog** in Scrum is essentially a list of tasks to complete in order to reach a goal.
It represents all the actions—small or big steps—that you need to take to move forward toward your aspirations.

However, it's not just a simple to-do list; the backlog is dynamic, evolving, and prioritized.

How to Build Your Backlog?

The first step is to define what you truly want to accomplish. Take the time to list your dreams, your projects, as well as all the actions needed to make them happen. For example, if your goal is to start a business, your backlog might include tasks like « write a business plan » « choose a company name » or « seek funding ». Once your list is created, you need to prioritize it. This is where Scrum stands out: instead of trying to do everything at once, you focus on the most important tasks that will have a direct impact on advancing your projects.

A good backlog should :

- Be detailed enough to be clear.
- Include all steps, even small daily tasks.
- Be flexible and regularly adjusted according to the progress of your projects.

2. The Sprint: A Period of Focus and Action

The **Sprint** is a key element of Scrum. It represents a fixed period of work (usually between one and four weeks) during which you focus on a subset of tasks from your backlog. The idea is to make intensive and focused progress on concrete actions, without getting distracted by longer-term goals. Each Sprint ends with a set of completed tasks, allowing you to track your progress and celebrate your successes at every step..

How to Structure Your Sprints? ?

When you start a Sprint, you need to set a specific and realistic goal you want to achieve by the end of the period. For example, if your long-term goal is to get fitter, a Sprint goal could be: « Work out 3 times a week for 4 weeks. » Once your goal is defined, select the most important tasks from your backlog that will help you reach it. Be precise about the time you will dedicate to each task so you don't get overwhelmed by tasks that are too big or too vague..

An effective Sprint should :

- Have a clear and precise goal.
- Focus on actions that bring you closest to your objective.
- Be time-boxed to stay motivating and measurable.

The idea is to create achievable steps, focus on immediate actions, and make adjustments at the end of each Sprint.

3. Retrospectives: Learning from Every Experience

One of the keys to Scrum is the **Retrospective**, which involves taking a step back at the end of each Sprint to reflect on what went well and what could be improved. It's a crucial moment for learning and adjustment.

Why Are Retrospectives Important ?

Retrospectives allow you to :

- Evaluate your process: Did you meet your objectives? Did you accomplish what you set out to do ?
- Identify obstacles encountered: What slowed you down? Why were some tasks left unfinished ?
- Implement corrective actions for the next Sprint: Based on your findings, you can adjust your methods, reorganize your Backlog, or revise your Sprint goal.

Retrospectives enable continuous improvement. They are an opportunity to celebrate your successes while making concrete improvements. They are not just an analysis tool: they are a motivation booster. They allow you to see how far you've come, celebrate your victories—even the smallest ones —and remind you why you started. It's a moment to recharge your mental and emotional energy to keep going.

An effective retrospective should :

- Be held regularly, after each Sprint.
- Be honest and constructive.
- Focus on concrete actions to improve your approach.

Take the time at the end of each Sprint for reflection. Imagine a reader who decided during their last Sprint to focus on improving their work-life balance. Their goal was to spend more time with family and reduce evening work hours. Here's what their retrospective might look like :

What went well :

- **Spending time with family:** I managed to organize family dinners three times a week, and I really enjoyed these moments of connection
- **Improvement in work hours:** I started shutting down my computer at 7 p.m. every day, which allowed me to free up time for other personal activities

What didn't work :

- **Weekend work time:** On weekends, I often struggled to completely detach from work and responded to professional emails on Saturdays
- **Deadline pressure:** Some work projects required more hours than expected, which prevented me from fully meeting my disconnection goals

Actions for the next Sprint :

- **Limit weekend emails:** I will set strict rules to no longer respond to professional emails after 7 p.m. and avoid checking them during the weekend
- **Reassess work priorities:** I will discuss with my colleagues the possibility of better organizing work to avoid overloads at the end of the week

4. Adaptation in Personal Life: Scrum in Everyday Life

When you apply Scrum to your personal life, you use a flexible yet structured framework to achieve your goals. You're not in a frantic race but in a process of continuous progress. Each Sprint, each Backlog, and each Retrospective become powerful tools to help you move forward.

Applying Scrum principles to your personal projects :

- Helps you clarify your goals.
- Allows you to track your progress in an organized way.
- Provides a framework to adjust your plans based on unforeseen events.
- Creates a dynamic of constant success, without pressure.

By integrating these three principles into your daily life, you will transform your aspirations into precise and measurable actions. You will be able to manage your personal projects with the agility and clarity that Scrum provides, while maintaining total flexibility to adapt at every stage of the process. Whether you have short-term projects or long-term life goals, Scrum for personal life is the tool you need to succeed.

2 - Organize Your Goals into a Backlog

Create a Clear and Detailed Backlog for Your Aspirations

The first key principle of Scrum, the Backlog, consists of creating a clear and organized list of actions needed to achieve a goal. For a personal project, the Backlog becomes a true action plan that evolves and guides you throughout your path to success.

Take the example of someone who wants to build muscle mass. Instead of setting a vague goal like « get muscular » the Backlog allows breaking it down into concrete and measurable actions. For instance, a backlog item could be « Buy whey protein » followed by other actions like « Join a gym » « Do 5 sets of 30 push-ups » « Do 4 sets of 20 squats » « Download a tracking app » and so on.

Each action should be sorted by value. You need to ask yourself this question: "If I complete this task, have I added real value to my goal?" Based on this reflection, you prioritize your actions from the most important to the least important. This way, you ensure that you focus your efforts on what has the greatest impact!

To track your project's progress, you can use an Excel file, like I do for my own Backlog and current Sprint. I keep this file open on my computer at all times, which allows me to check it every day and stay focused on my priorities.

Let's take the example again of the person who wants to build muscle mass, one of their goals. Their Backlog could look like this:
I have sorted and listed the tasks in order of importance, from the most crucial to the least priority.

To get muscular	
Buy whey protein	
Sign up at the gym	
Do 5 sets of 40 push-ups per day	
Do 4 sets of 30 squats per day	
Download a fitness tracking app	

Now let's add a second goal, just as personal but of a different nature: a trip to New York. We will add this goal to the backlog with the following tasks :

- Define the travel dates
- Obtain the necessary documents (VISA)
- Book the flight
- Book accommodation
- Plan activities and visits
- Pack the suitcase

In the same way, we will add it to our Backlog, which will then look like this :

To get muscular
Buy whey protein
Sign up at the gym
Do 5 sets of 40 push-ups per day
Do 4 sets of 30 squats per day
Download a fitness tracking app

Take a trip to New York
Set the travel dates
Obtain travel documents
Book the flight
Book the accommodation
Plan activities and sightseeing
Pack the suitcase

You'll notice that I assign a **different color to each goal** in my backlog. This is not just an aesthetic choice. Each color is intentionally selected based on what the goal evokes for me. For example, I might use green for a health or balance-related goal, blue for a writing project that brings me serenity, or red for an ambition that excites me and drives me to action.

This color-goal association is based on the principle of emotional visualization mentioned in the chapter about the law of attraction. It **adds a symbolic, almost intuitive dimension to your backlog**. Colors activate specific emotions, strengthen your connection to each goal, and make them easier to remember. At a glance, you feel what that goal means to you.

This transforms your backlog into a tool that is not only organized but also inspiring. It's no longer just a to-do list: it becomes a living, colorful, vibrant representation of what you are building — an emotional map of your aspirations.

A personal goals backlog evolves based on your progress, priorities, and circumstances. Here's how it can transform over time :

1 - Adding New Goals: You can add new goals as your priorities or desires change. For example, after reaching a fitness goal, you might decide to add another one, such as going on a trip or learning a new skill.

2 - Task Prioritization: Depending on the urgency and impact of each action, you can readjust the priority of tasks in your Backlog. This process of reevaluation allows you to focus your energy on what is most important at any given time.

3 - Reviewing Objectives: Over time, some objectives may lose their relevance. You can reevaluate, adjust, or even remove them to better align with your current needs.

4 - Adapting to External Constraints: Unexpected events (such as changes in your personal or professional situation) may require revisiting certain tasks or adjusting objectives to make them more achievable.

5 - Tracking Progress and Adjusting: After each action phase, you can reassess your progress and adjust the next steps based on the results achieved.

In summary, the Backlog becomes a true guide that helps you transform your dreams into concrete actions. It is this method that enables you to focus on what matters most and stay on course to achieve your goals, whether personal, professional, or otherwise.

How to Prioritize Tasks for Each Project

Once your goals are defined and your tasks are well structured in your **Backlog**, the next step is to prioritize those tasks. This is where the **Eisenhower Matrix** comes into play—a powerful method to help you decide what truly deserves your attention. This matrix sorts your actions into four categories based on their urgency and importance. By combining it with your values (from the previous chapter), you will be able to focus your energy on what really matters to you.

Once your backlog is defined, you still need to know where to start. This is where a strategic tool comes in: the Eisenhower Matrix.

The Eisenhower Matrix: A Simple Yet Effective Method

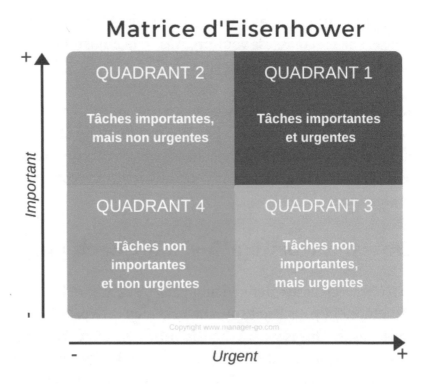

The Eisenhower Matrix is divided into four quadrants, each representing a different level of priority. Here is how it works:

Quadrant 1 (Urgent / Important): These are tasks that must be done immediately. They have a major impact on your goals and cannot be delayed.

Quadrant 2 (Urgent / Not Important): These tasks demand your attention now but do not have a significant impact on your long-term projects. They are often interruptions.

Quadrant 3 (Not Urgent / Important): These tasks have real value potential but no immediate time constraints. They are actions to plan and execute strategically.

Quadrant 4 (Not Urgent / Not Important): These tasks bring little or no value to your goals. They can be postponed or even removed from your Backlog.
Step 1: Categorize each task in the matrix

Let's take the example of a person whose goals are to **build muscle mass** and to **travel to New York.** We will apply the Eisenhower Matrix to prioritize the tasks in their Backlog.

To get muscular	
Buy whey protein	**3 (Not Urgent / Important)**
Sign up at the gym	**1 (Urgent / Important)**
Do 5 sets of 40 push-ups per day	**3 (Not Urgent / Important)**
Do 4 sets of 30 squats per day	**3 (Not Urgent / Important)**
Download a fitness tracking app	**4 (Not Urgent / Not Important)**

Take a trip to New York	
Set the travel dates	**1 (Urgent / Important)**
Obtain travel documents	**3 (Not Urgent / Important)**
Book the flight	**1 (Urgent / Important)**
Book the accommodation	**3 (Not Urgent / Important)**
Plan activities and sightseeing	**3 (Not Urgent / Important)**
Pack the suitcase	**4 (Not Urgent / Not Important)**

Miscellaneous	
Reply to a non-urgent email	**4 (Not Urgent / Not Important)**
Organize a get-together with friends	**4 (Not Urgent / Not Important)**

In this example, you will notice that **tasks with a direct impact on your goals** are placed in quadrants 1 and 3. For instance, « Sign up at the gym » and « Book the flight to New York » are urgent and important—they need to be addressed immediately. On the other hand, tasks like "Reply to a non-urgent email" are less important and can be postponed.

We can therefore reorganize our backlog as follows:

To get muscular	
Sign up at the gym	**1 (Urgent / Important)**
Buy whey protein	**3 (Not Urgent / Important)**
Do 5 sets of 40 push-ups per day	**3 (Not Urgent / Important)**
Do 4 sets of 30 squats per day	**3 (Not Urgent / Important)**
Download a fitness tracking app	**4 (Not Urgent / Not Important)**

Take a trip to New York	
Set the travel dates	**1 (Urgent / Important)**
Book the flight	**1 (Urgent / Important)**
Obtain travel documents	**3 (Not Urgent / Important)**
Book the accommodation	**3 (Not Urgent / Important)**
Plan activities and sightseeing	**3 (Not Urgent / Important)**
Pack the suitcase	**4 (Not Urgent / Not Important)**

Miscellaneous	
Reply to a non-urgent email	**4 (Not Urgent / Not Important)**
Organize a get-together with friends	**4 (Not Urgent / Not Important)**

Step 2: Analyze and Act According to Priority

Once you have classified your tasks, it is essential to understand how to act on each of them. Here is what you should do for each quadrant:

Quadrant 1: Urgent / Important
These are crucial tasks that have a direct impact on your projects. They cannot be postponed and must be done immediately. For example, if your flight to New York must be booked before a certain date, you absolutely need to take care of it quickly.

Quadrant 2: Urgent / Not Important
Tasks in this quadrant require your attention now, but they don't have a real impact on your long-term projects. They are often distractions or external requests. For example, a phone call to confirm an appointment can be urgent but not fundamental to advancing your dreams.

Quadrant 3: Not Urgent / Important
These are strategic tasks that help you move toward your long-term goals but don't require immediate urgency. For

example, buying Whey protein to complement your nutrition plan is essential to reach your muscle gain goals, but it's not urgent.

Quadrant 4: Not Urgent / Not Important
These tasks bring little value to your projects and have no time constraints. For example, organizing a party with friends can be enjoyable, but it should not be a priority when you have goals to achieve.

Step 3: Continuous Re-evaluation

Prioritizing tasks is not a fixed process. You need to regularly re-evaluate your tasks according to how your projects evolve. As you progress, some tasks may move from one quadrant to another. For example, a task initially in quadrant 3 can become urgent if a deadline approaches.

Tip: Take a few minutes each week to reorganize your Backlog based on changing priorities. This will help you stay on track and ensure your actions remain aligned with your long-term goals.

Practical Exercise No. 6: Create Your First Personal Backlog

1. **Choose a clear goal you want to achieve within the next 3 months.**
(Examples: lose 5 kilos, start a blog, learn Spanish, create a source of passive income...)
2. **Take a sheet of paper or open a digital document (Excel, Notion, Trello, etc.).**
3. **List all the concrete actions that come to mind to reach this goal.**
Don't censor yourself: write down everything that seems useful, even if some tasks appear small or vague.
4. **Sort your actions in two steps :**
    *   Remove unnecessary or irrelevant tasks.
    *   Prioritize the remaining tasks: from the most impactful to the least urgent.

3 - Sprints: Taking Action the Agile Way

Breaking Down Big Ambitions into Short-Term Concrete Actions

The Importance of Breaking Things Down

When you have a big dream or a long-term ambition, it's easy to feel overwhelmed by the scale of the project. That's why it's essential to break down those big ambitions into concrete, manageable short-term actions. This is exactly what we do in a **Scrum Sprint**.

Sprints are a key concept in the Scrum framework. They allow you to break ambitious goals into actionable, achievable steps in the short term. Rather than getting overwhelmed by a large project, a Sprint helps you focus your efforts on specific, measurable actions that can be completed within a limited timeframe.

What Is a Scrum Sprint ?

A Sprint is a fixed period of focused work—typically between 1 and 4 weeks (though I recommend two weeks as the ideal length)—during which a team concentrates on a specific set of tasks taken from the Backlog. In this case, the team is you!

The goal of a Sprint is to deliver a concrete, measurable result by the end of the period.

The timebox is essential: it helps prevent procrastination and allows you to quickly see the results of your efforts.

Sprint Goal

The main objective of a Sprint is to focus on specific actions defined in your Backlog and complete them in a way that brings tangible value to your project. Ask yourself this simple question: *What will I have concretely accomplished in two weeks?* That's the essence of a Sprint.

The Fibonacci Points Method

In the Scrum methodology, instead of measuring the duration of a task, we use points to estimate its size or difficulty. One of the most common approaches is the Fibonacci sequence, which uses numbers such as: 1, **2, 3, 5, 8, 13, 21**, etc. These numbers help indicate the relative effort required to complete each task while maintaining flexibility in estimation.

Scrum points don't measure time—**they compare the complexity of tasks to one another**. For example, a task rated at 8 points will be more complex or effort-intensive than a 3-point task, but less so than a 13-point task.

And now, let's get to the game-changing part: how do you turn your big ideas into concrete actions?

Let's see how to apply this to your personal projects.
Take, for example, two items from your Backlog: **building muscle mass** and **planning a trip to New York**. These

are ambitious goals and may seem overwhelming at first. However, by breaking them down into short-term concrete actions within a Sprint, you'll be able to achieve them step by step.

Creating a Sprint from the Backlog

Let's take the highest-priority tasks from your Backlog and organize them into a Sprint.

Remember, the Backlog contains important tasks related to your goals, prioritized based on their value and impact.

Sprint 1: Build Muscle Mass and Plan a Trip to New York

Sprint Goal: Take concrete steps to start a fitness program and organize the first stages of your trip to New York.

Sprint Tasks :

1. Sign up for the gym (Urgent/Important) – 2 points
Description: Find a gym near your home, compare options, and sign up to start training your body

2. Book the flight to New York (Urgent/Important) – 3 points
Description: Search for the best flight deals and book one that matches your travel dates

3. Set the travel dates (Urgent/Important) – 1 point

4. Buy whey protein (Not urgent/Important) – 1 point
Description: Research and purchase whey protein online or at a specialty store

5. Prepare travel documents (Not urgent/Important) – 3 points
Description: Check entry requirements for New York (visa, valid passport, etc.) and begin gathering the necessary documents.

Sprint 1: Start Strength Training and Plan the Trip			
	Goal	**Points**	
Sign up for the gym	**To get muscular**	2	**1 (Urgent / Important)**
Book the flight	**New York**	3	**1 (Urgent / Important)**
Set the travel dates	**New York**	1	**1 (Urgent / Important)**
Buy whey protein	**To get muscular**	1	**3 (Not Urgent / Important)**
Obtain travel documents	**New York**	3	**3 (Not Urgent / Important)**

Tracking and Evaluation:

At the end of this 2-week Sprint, you should have completed tasks totaling at least 10 points. This will allow you to assess the overall progress of your project. If some tasks are not completed, they should be carried over to the next Sprints, with points adjusted if needed.

Adaptation and Adjustment:

Sprints are flexible. At the end of each Sprint, you'll have the opportunity to review your priorities, **adjust your tasks, and evaluate your progress**. The key is to focus on the actions that bring you closer to your goals, while remaining agile and adaptable to unexpected changes.

Conclusion:

Scrum Sprints are an excellent way to break down your big ambitions into concrete, manageable short-term actions. By applying this method to your personal projects and using Fibonacci points to estimate the effort required, you can maintain a **clear vision of your priorities** and stay on track with your goals. Each Sprint helps you make tangible progress, stay motivated, and achieve your long-term objectives, step by step

Practical Exercise No. 7: Start Your First Personal Sprint

1. Choose a clear goal

Choose a personal project that you truly want to move forward with, one that's in your backlog (e.g., writing an article, getting back into fitness, reorganizing your workspace, creating an offer...). And write it down: « My sprint goal: _____ »

2. Build your sprint backlog

List all the actions needed to make progress on this goal over the next 15 days. Then estimate each task using **effort points** (based on the Fibonacci sequence: 1, 2, 3, 5, 8...).

3. Set your capacity

Decide how many points you believe you can reasonably complete during this sprint.

4. Start the sprint

Start today. Each day, track your progress: record the completed tasks, the points achieved, and any potential blockers.

Track your progress and adjust your actions throughout the sprints

Scrum is not just a planning method. It is a dynamic framework designed to help you make continuous progress. When you apply Scrum principles to your personal projects, tracking your progress becomes a key management tool—not just a simple activity report. It's this tracking, combined with regular adjustments, that enables you to move efficiently toward your goals while staying aligned with your priorities.

Understanding the Logic of the Sprint

In Scrum, a sprint is a focused action period during which you commit to completing a set of tasks from your backlog. These tasks are chosen based on their importance, urgency, and the value they bring to your goal.

For each selected task, you assign an estimate in points using the Fibonacci sequence (1, 2, 3, 5, 8, 13, etc.). This system helps measure the relative effort or complexity of a task without falling into the trap of fixed or unrealistic durations. The goal of a sprint is to complete a certain number of points within an action cycle, aiming for concrete and measurable progress.

Why Tracking Is Essential

Tracking the progress of a sprint means becoming aware, day by day, of what is moving forward, what is stagnating, and what adjustments need to be made. This allows you to :

- Recognize the progress made compared to your initial commitments.
- Identify blockages or recurring friction points.
- Observe your own habits and behaviors.
- Assess your actual capacity to accomplish a given volume of tasks.

This helps you avoid falling into the illusion of constant action, favoring progress that is firmly grounded in reality.

The Power of the Retrospective

At the end of each sprint, a time for reflection is essential. This is called the retrospective. It is a moment of analysis, perspective, and clarity. It is not about judgment, but about learning from experience.

Here are three simple questions to ask yourself :

1. What went well during this sprint ?
2. What difficulties or obstacles did I encounter ?
3. What can I improve or do differently in the next sprint ?

These answers will help you better understand yourself, strengthen what works, and correct what slows your progress. This might involve better prioritization, adjusting the number of tasks chosen, or simply changing your approach to certain actions.

Adjust to Progress

The purpose of a sprint is precisely to offer you short learning cycles. Thanks to tracking and retrospectives, you can modify your course without losing sight of your overall goal.

This adjustment can take several forms :

- Reorganizing your backlog according to new priorities.
- Reducing the volume of actions to stay effective without burning out.
- Changing certain tasks to better fit your current situation.
- Taking into account new personal constraints or opportunities.

This process of continuous adaptation is what distinguishes simple planning from a true agile approach. You allow yourself to evolve based on your own learnings, without locking yourself into a rigid structure.

In summary

Tracking your progress through sprints and adjusting your actions is a core practice to turn your goals into lasting results. It is through this regularity, honesty with yourself, and flexibility in action that you will develop a momentum for success.

Sprint after sprint, you learn, you adjust, you progress. And each step brings you closer to your dreams.

Part 4: Aligning Action, Perseverance, and Results

1 - Dream Big, Act Concretely

Finding the Balance Between Visualization and Execution to Manifest Your Goals

Every success begins with a dream. An inner drive. An intuition that life can be bigger, richer, more vibrant. This dream is the starting point. It's the spark that lights the flame, the reason you want to get up in the morning full of energy and passion. But this spark, as beautiful as it is, is not enough on its own.

Dreaming big is essential. But acting concretely is just as important. This chapter invites you to understand how these two forces — imagination and action — don't oppose each other but rather complement one another. Together, they form a powerful duo capable of transforming any goal into tangible reality.

Dreaming: The Fuel of Transformation

The greatest inventions, the most beautiful stories, and the most inspiring journeys all began with a dream. Visualizing your future is giving your mind a clear direction, a destination. When you intensely dream about a goal, you create a mental image so strong that it begins to influence your emotions, decisions, and behaviors.

Neuroscience studies have shown that the brain activates the same neural areas when visualizing an action as when actually performing it.

This means imagination can train your mind like a muscle. By regularly visualizing your goals, you prepare yourself mentally. You begin to believe they are possible... then inevitable.

But beware: dreaming does not mean escaping reality. It's not a refuge, but a compass.

I am a big dreamer; sometimes I imagine myself sailing, owning my own boat — it's an idea I like. By thinking about it often, I recently took the boating license, which is already a first step! By visualizing this goal, I gradually live toward achieving it.

Acting: The Bridge Between Idea and Reality

A dream without action remains a beautiful fiction.

It is by laying the first stones, even small ones, that you build your project. Too often, we get stuck because of fear of imperfection, fear of failure, or impostor syndrome. Yet every step, even clumsy, has value. It's the momentum that counts, not perfection.

The agile approach, originally from the software development world, teaches us that we can build big projects by moving step by step — testing, correcting, learning. Applying this logic to your personal goals means giving yourself permission to experiment without pressure, to progress without waiting for everything to be « perfect ».

Don't try to plan everything at once. Choose the next smallest action that brings you closer to your dream, and do it today.

The balance to cultivate daily

It's easy to fall into one of two extremes :
- **The chronic dreamer**, who imagines extraordinary lives without ever taking action.
- **The exhausted doer**, who acts without direction, ticking boxes without real motivation.

The ideal is to nourish your dreams every day while making concrete progress. Alternate between moments of inspiration and moments of action. Make your schedule a balance between the two: 5 minutes of visualization in the morning, followed by a concrete task. A reflection session on Sunday evening, then micro-goals for the week.

You are the captain of a ship that needs both a map and oars.

Practical Exercise No. 8 :

1. **Visualization**
   Write your dream with sensory precision: what you see, hear, feel, touch, and experience emotionally.

2. **List of Actions**
   Break down this dream into 3 simple and accessible actions. For example: find a mentor, sign up for a course, talk about your project with a close friend.

3. **Immediate Commitment**
   Choose ONE action to do within 24 hours. No matter the size. Movement is what counts.

4. **Create a Ritual**
   Every morning or evening, take 5 minutes to revisit your vision and 10 minutes to advance your project. Make it a habit.

2 - Turning ideas into measurable results

Using SMART Goals and Simple Metrics to Track Your Progress

In the whirlwind of daily life, many ideas emerge without ever materializing. The difference between a fleeting inspiration and a progressing project often lies in the clarity of objectives and how they are broken down. This is where the personal backlog comes in: a living dashboard where you structure your intentions into concrete tasks.

But not all tasks are equal. For the backlog to become a true engine of transformation, it is essential that each item is formulated in a **SMART** way — Specific, Measurable, Achievable, Realistic, and Time-bound.

The **SMART** framework is a simple yet powerful tool to formulate effective goals. Here's what it means:

- **S for Specific** → The goal must be clear, precise, and unambiguous.
  Example: « Write a book » becomes « Write a 100-page ebook on personal agility »
- **M for Measurable** → You should be able to tell if you are making progress or not.
  Example: « Exercise » becomes « Do 3 sessions of 30 minutes per week »

- **A for Achievable** → It should be ambitious but possible with your current resources.
  No point aiming for 1 million subscribers in 1 month if you're just starting out.
- **R for Realistic** → Align your goals with your reality: schedule, energy, resources.
  A single parent won't plan for 4 hours of training per day..
- **T for Time-bound** → Give a date or deadline.
  Example: "Launch my website by May 30th."

OSMART Goals: A Filter for Clarity

In an agile approach to life, every task entered into the backlog should meet these criteria. This framework prevents vague formulations like "getting back in shape" or "starting a project." These intentions are legitimate, but without precision, they provide no clear direction.

On the other hand, a well-defined task might look like:
→ "Complete the outline for chapter 3 by Sunday evening"
→ "Create a cover visual in 30 minutes using an online tool"

A backlog filled with SMART tasks offers an instant view of your priorities and makes decision-making easier. It becomes more than a list: a concrete and engaging roadmap.

Measuring Progress, Even Without Obsessing Over Numbers

The value of SMART tasks also lies in their measurability. Not to fall into excessive quantification, but to maintain a

simple and honest dialogue with yourself.
Have you done what you planned?
Are the deadlines realistic?
Do you need to adjust the pace or workload?

These small regular checks create a link between your intentions and your actions, between your dreams and their realization.

The Backlog as a Reflection of Personal Growth

Over time, the backlog becomes a mirror of your journey. Tasks that are abandoned, postponed, or reformulated tell a story: one of changing priorities, growing clarity, and learning to think in concrete results.

Far from being fixed, this backlog is a dynamic, flexible, living tool. It supports you in turning your ideas into action, while allowing you to keep an overview.

3 - Staying Motivated Despite Obstacles

Cultivating Emotional and Mental Resilience in the Face of the Unexpected

Every journey, whether personal or professional, is marked by unforeseen events, setbacks, and even discouragement. It would be unrealistic to believe that a path of self-fulfillment, no matter how well planned, can unfold without bumps along the way. The key is not to avoid obstacles... but to learn how to navigate them with calmness and inner strength.

Obstacles Are Part of the Path

It's natural to experience moments of doubt, fatigue, or discouragement. These moments do not mean you have failed. Often, they are signs that you have stepped out of your comfort zone and are therefore progressing.

Life projects are not built in a straight line. They are living journeys made of cycles. Progress is not always visible, but it is built deeply, during periods of silent effort or apparent setbacks.

Resilience: Between Emotion and Clarity

Being resilient doesn't mean enduring everything without reaction. It means acknowledging your feelings without being overwhelmed by them. It means accepting temporary failure without letting it undermine your worth or your goal.

Resilience is the ability to return again and again, flexibly, to your course. It is learning to pause without giving up. It is recognizing that every detour can hold a lesson. It is understanding that sometimes, slowing down is also moving forward.

Keeping the Inner Fire Alive

Staying motivated doesn't depend solely on iron willpower. It also relies on regularly fueling your mental and emotional energy. Visualizing your progress, revisiting your deep intentions, celebrating small victories: these are concrete ways to maintain your momentum.

A well-organized backlog alone is not enough. You also need to nurture the flame that drives you to act. To remember why you started. To reconnect with the meaning behind your journey. Because it is this meaning, even more than immediate results, that allows you to persevere over time.

Turning Failure into a Springboard

Failures are not endings but stages. Resilience invites you to adopt a dynamic view of your difficulties. Every unexpected event is a disguised opportunity to better know yourself, adjust your strategy, and strengthen your commitment.

What you go through shapes you. Moments of tension sharpen your discernment, strengthen your clarity, and develop your inner agility. Over time, what you thought was a wall reveals itself as a passage to a stronger and more lucid version of yourself.

The Secret: Never Break the Link with Your Goal

Even in the most uncertain moments, keep a connection—no matter how fragile—with your goal. This link can be an image, a phrase, or an intention written in a notebook. It becomes your anchor in storms. It reminds you that you move forward for a reason greater than the difficulty of the moment.

Staying motivated is not about being invulnerable. It's about knowing how to draw on your inner resources when external conditions falter. It's about showing gentle, steady, patient strength.

4 - Agile Discipline: Sustaining Momentum Over the Long Term

Creating Routines and Habits That Support Your Vision

Motivation is a spark. Discipline, on the other hand, is the fire that keeps burning long after the initial enthusiasm has faded. In an agile approach, discipline is not a rigid constraint but a flexible framework that supports you daily and helps you move forward even when motivation fluctuates.

Discipline as a Commitment to Yourself

Too often, discipline is associated with harshness or deprivation. Yet, when chosen consciously, it becomes an act of kindness towards yourself. It is a freely accepted structure, a way to stay true to your deepest aspirations.

In personal agility, discipline takes the form of light, intentional routines that facilitate action and reduce unnecessary decisions. It's not about acting mechanically but creating an environment where your goals are more likely to be naturally realized.

Routines That Support the Vision

Your vision only makes sense if it is rooted in repeated actions. For this, routines are your allies. Each day, each week, you can rely on a chosen rhythm that suits your energy and priorities.

These can be simple rituals: a daily visualization session, a weekly moment to plan your tasks in your backlog, a monthly retrospective to observe your progress. These rituals give coherence and continuity to your efforts.

Agility and Consistency: A Subtle Balance

Personal agility doesn't mean acting on constant impulse. Rather, it invites you to combine flexibility and regularity. It's a constant balancing act: holding a course without clinging to a single way to get there.

When the unexpected happens, agile discipline allows you to reassess your priorities without guilt. It offers you landmarks rather than obligations. It helps you stay active, rather than being overwhelmed by life's uncertainties.

The Power of Micro-Actions

Maintaining momentum doesn't always require great effort. Often, it's the small repeated gestures that make all the difference. Updating a task, rereading your goal, dedicating five minutes to a neglected project... These micro-actions nurture a dynamic of movement.

Agile discipline values these small, steady steps. It recognizes that progress is rarely spectacular, but always the result of an intention maintained over time.

From Rigor to Fluidity

Over time, the routines you've put in place become almost invisible. They integrate into your daily life like a background rhythm. It's no longer an effort: it becomes second nature. And that's precisely where the magic happens.

Your discipline is no longer perceived as a burden, but as a natural support for your freedom to act. You no longer struggle to move forward: you are carried by a system you have built, step by step, with intelligence and self-respect.

Conclusion : You are the Scrum Master of your life

Throughout this book, you have explored a powerful idea: taking back the reins of your life through simple principles inspired by agility, creative visualization, and intentional action.

To dream big, to turn your ideas into concrete goals, to learn from your experiences, to cultivate resilience, to establish flexible discipline... each chapter has been a step toward a personal transformation that is both structured and deeply human.

But at the core, no tool, no model, no method can replace the true engine of your progress: you.

You are the one who defines the vision.
You are the one who prioritizes, moves forward, and adjusts.
You are the Scrum Master of your own life.

This role is not that of an authoritarian leader but of a caring guide. Someone who knows how to create space to grow, to make mistakes, and to start over. Someone who facilitates change, who lights the way even when the path seems uncertain.

You have within you all the resources necessary to shape a life that reflects you, a life that inspires you. By applying these principles with consistency and adaptability, you are not simply chasing your dreams: **you are building them day by day, sprint by sprint.**

And if tomorrow the winds change, if your priorities evolve, you will welcome this movement with confidence because you will have learned to steer your course with clarity and flexibility.

So don't wait for perfect conditions. Don't wait to know everything. Start. Move forward. Adjust. Celebrate every progress.

Because the greatest adventure there is, is to become fully the actor of your own life.

And you are ready.

"It's not the wind that decides your destination, but the direction you give to your sail"
Jim Rohn

Acknowledgments

Writing this book has been a deeply personal journey, both exciting and transformative.

I want to express my gratitude to everyone who, near or far, contributed to the birth of this project.
Thank you to my family, the cornerstone of my balance: to my children, whom I love more than anything in the world, to my brother and parents for their unwavering presence.

To my friends, those kind voices who whispered, « Proud of you » thank you simply for being there.

My gratitude also goes to those who were catalysts in my own transformation: my mentors, loved ones, and especially Éloïse, Raphaël, Sarah, and Martin. Thank you to Laurent for passionately sharing with me the foundations of the Scrum methodology.

To all those whose words, silences, or simple exchanges nourished my reflections and opened new perspectives, thank you.

A huge thank you to those who inspired me to connect two seemingly opposite worlds: the rigor of Scrum and the magic of the law of attraction.

And finally, thank you to you, dear reader. If this book is in your hands today, it is no accident. May these pages help you reconnect with your deepest dreams and guide you toward aligned, clear, and confident action.

I dedicate this book to my sister, taken too soon, whose absence still lights my way.
With all my gratitude.

A quick note before we part...

If this book has inspired you, helped you, or simply made you feel good, I would be very grateful if you could take a moment to **leave a review on the platform** where you discovered it.

Your feedback, even a short one, helps other readers make their choice... and allows me to keep sharing the passion that drives me deeply.

Thank you from the bottom of my heart for your support.

Author's Note

This book is the result of a long journey, both personal and professional. For over twenty years, I have worked in the field of information technology, where I've had the opportunity to support numerous projects, help teams transform, and experience the challenges of change from the inside.

My passion for agility and knowledge sharing naturally led me to train and become certified as a Scrum Master. Very quickly, I felt the need to share this approach—teaching it to students as well as to professionals in career transition, seeking clarity, guidance, and effectiveness.

Through these pages, I offer you the lessons that have profoundly transformed the way I think, act... and dream. Every idea, every method, every example you'll find here is based on real-life experience. Nothing has been copied or automatically generated. This is not a compilation of generic content or PLR (Private Label Rights) material, but a sincere work, written from the heart and with a deep desire to help.

I wanted to build a bridge between the discipline of a proven framework like Scrum and the power of personal vision. Between structure and inspiration. Between dreaming and doing.

If this book brings you even a spark of insight, a shift in perspective, or a new way of approaching your goals, then it will have fulfilled its purpose.

Thank you for joining me on this journey—through these words, and perhaps, toward your own transformation.

Made in United States
Cleveland, OH
27 May 2025